What people are saying about
Effective Time Management for High Achievers

"Structured people need a system to keep their time on track. Andrew Martin's book is a quick and easy way to build that. It won't take much time to read, understand and use and it will save you hours!"
Terrence Chermak
Chief Executive Officer, Britannia Mills LTD

"Andrew has written an up to date time management tool that ranks up there with David Allen's *Getting Things Done* in a more efficient presentation." A couple of hours spent absorbing this book will change your life."
Gary Rochlin
Chief Executive Officer, Blue Sky Energy, Inc.

"I have often wondered how Andrew was able to get so much accomplished while simultaneously pursuing multiple ventures. He has a great knack for finding order in complexity and for discovering wondrous kernels of wisdom."
Frank Nemiroff
Chief Executive Officer, Nemco Food Products, Inc.

"Andrew is one of the sharpest, process oriented, businessmen I know."
David Golob
Chief Executive Officer, Microcom Technologies, Inc.

Dedicated to all who have that nagging feeling that something else needs to get done, and can't remember what it is.

Effective Time Management for High Achievers

By

Andrew T. Martin

With special thanks to

Balanced Center Living
A philosophy of seven guiding principles to a better quality of life
www.BalancedCenterLiving.com

Balanced Center Living
4426 Pepperwood Ave
Long Beach, CA 90808 USA
www.balancedcenterliving.com

ISBN 978-0-9827233-2-6

Contents

Prelude

"I just don't have the time to do everything I need to do."

"I have always wanted to do that but can't seem to make the time."

"I don't have the time for a social life."

"There's just one last thing I have to do before I leave."

Do these sentiments sound familiar? If so, it is likely that you are a high achiever. As such, it is a part of your psychology to want to succeed at everything you do, and to continually seek new challenges to conquer. If you fit this description, read on and discover a tried and true method of time management that will change your life forever. One word of caution: effective time management is a serious endeavor that will require your whole-hearted commitment and active participation in order to succeed. I promise you that **Effective Time Management for High Achievers** will produce results if you are committed to following each of the steps outlined in this process:

1. Build an Action Plan
2. Take Advantage of Existing Habits
3. Use Your Energy Wisely
4. Build a Day Plan
5. Schedule Tasks
6. Organize
7. Keep Your Schedule Current
8. Prioritize Objectives
9. Make Time To Review
10. Effectively Handle Interruptions
11. Keep The Commitment
12. Reward The Success

By following the instructions, you will find the preoccupation of wondering, "what else needed to be done" will virtually disappear. You will also find it possible to schedule time to take care of those projects that never seem to get crossed off the task list. One day a realization will come over you that you are all caught up on what you wanted to do: no last minute details to finish, no urgent surprises to handle.

I know these claims seem wondrous at the moment, but I assure you there is no fantasy in these statements. Many high achievers, all of whom make similar claims of finding "hours per day," have successfully implemented this time management program and continue to live by its teachings and principles.

A Story from the Author

I am an entrepreneurial business owner, at times involved with several businesses. As such, I never seem to have time enough to complete the projects I wish to complete. However, I do have my projects organized and prioritized in alignment with my business and personal goals. As a result, I am considered by most to be a successful businessman with a balanced life and a healthy future. While I still do not have enough time to pursue all of the ideas and opportunities that surround my life, most people that know me would tell you I am the most productive person they know. I don't think this has anything to do with intelligence, upbringing, attention span or energy: I feel that the secret to productivity lies within a time management system.

As a result of my entrepreneurial spirit, I love to be involved in the creation of a business. In fact, I make the time to be involved in so many different projects that I would most assuredly go insane if I was forced to manage all my activities without an effective time management system. It was not too long ago when I was without a practical and effective time management system.

2

Going back a few years, I can vividly remember a time when the business was growing rapidly and everything about my professional and personal life seemed out of control. I was desperately trying to juggle all of those seemingly important items all at once. I was a generalist at all duties and a master of none. Physical and mental health was jeopardized as I incessantly pushed harder to accomplish what I felt was needed on any given day. Then a revelation came to me on the day that would change my life forever.

While on an airplane, I began to reevaluate my personal and professional life. I wondered if things would ever get better, or if this was all I could expect from being a business owner. I asked myself if I should give up, or if I should try harder? I knew that I controlled my future, and I knew that I could succeed with enough effort. At that point I made a decision to reprioritize my life and take control of managing my efforts. Coincidentally, there was a brief article about time management in a magazine I was flipping through, so I made time to read the article while on the airplane. After reading the article it was clear to me that the key to balance in my life would be effective time management.

I began to gather time management information through books, seminars, magazine articles, audio and videotapes. I found a wealth of information in each of the programs, but I was not successful at implementing any of them. It seemed that I could not get ahead of my workload in order to get scheduled and then stay there. After all the information gathering and failed attempts at scheduling, I was still working twelve hour days from Monday through Saturday and I was working most Sundays as well.

Once again, I found myself on an airplane reevaluating my personal and professional life when I realized that I had built a devastating cycle that would prevent me from accomplishing what I wanted out of life. This time I asked myself, "Why I was not acting to affect change in my behavior?" I concluded that the time management programs I had been experimenting with were not designed for people with my motivations, and it was at that moment

I decided to design a time management system that would work for me, a high achiever. Work began immediately and an outline was completed before touching down at my destination that day.

I began my time management efforts and kept a record of how much time I was able to gain through using the system and improving the time management system over time. This time I was able to stick with the program after making a strong commitment to changing my life for the better. After one year of fine tuning the time management system into what is presented in this program, I was able to generate an additional two hours per day of productive work time and I was able to altogether stop working on Sunday. When I added up the time-savings per year I was amazed: in total, 832 hours, or nearly 13 additional sixty-hour workweeks per year!

Shortly thereafter I began issuing the time management program to the management staff at my company, all high achiever personality types. To my surprise, they were able to implement the program within a couple of months and found average time-savings on the order of six to ten hours per week! That is when I knew that this time management system really works.

I know it seems fantastic to think that a simple time management program can make such a difference in one's life. However, a committed high achiever can accomplish many things that seem fantastic. Consider: if you are a high achiever, you have the opportunity to invest a few dollars and a few weeks into a customized time management system that will generate potentially hundreds of thousands of dollars and years of time for you in the future. This is probably one of the best opportunities ever presented to you.

While I cannot guarantee you will encounter the same results as I have, I can promise that you will be an excellent time manager after successfully completing this program. And who knows, this program may just change your life too.

Foreword

A program designed to help high achievers with the time management process should be brief and direct. This guide will not waste your time with concepts and thoughts unrelated to effective time management. All of the information in this program is valuable in some way. Often, the information is presented in a specific order to allow the reader the experience of contemplating the application of the topic to his/her own life experiences prior to moving on to the next step in the time management system. The process of understanding what is being read is only a small part of the time management system. A much larger part of the time management process is developing self-awareness while designing a customized process that suits your individual time management needs. This program will not benefit all people equally, however the high achiever who takes the time to really understand themselves and their goals will create an incredible value from this time management program.

    This guide is presented in a series of brief steps that are organized to best enable the successful implementation of the time management program. It is not recommended that any step be skipped, cut short, or executed out of order. High achievers will want to read ahead, or perhaps read the entire guide and then go about implementing the steps. Please do not attempt to do this; you will most assuredly fail if you do. Years of experience with the time management development process have proven that those who try to cheat the system will not succeed. High achievers want it all right away; this author understands that better than you know, however you must fight the urges to proceed at a quickened pace. The time frames outlined in the time management process are specifically designed with the most efficiency. Hurrying the steps along will only cause failure in implementing the process.

To maximize your success, follow each of the chapter instructions in detail. After just a few weeks, you will find yourself able to manage your time, make free time, and concentrate on the project at hand with ease and comfort. Perhaps more importantly, you will find yourself no longer wondering if everything is getting done. Not only will your mind be clearer, but you will also find that there is free time available to think and grow and enjoy your accomplishments. You will rest easy knowing that your priorities are being handled completely and efficiently, and that your direction in life is clear. You will have control of your destiny, and you will have the time to make the correct decisions at the right times that will make you increasingly more successful and fulfilled.

Behavior Modification:

Effective time management cannot be turned on or off when convenient. It is a set of skills and behaviors that become a pervasive part of one's professional and personal life. Make not mistake in judgment, after committing to and completing this time management program, you will be changed for the rest of your life. And, like anything truly worthwhile, this time management program will require significant effort at first, until the system is mastered. You will not be able to read through this guide and magically manage time better. Quite to the contrary, it will take commitment, hard work and relentless attention to forcing proper behaviors at all times. With all this effort, you would expect the payoff to be substantial, and it is. The payoff will be a life-changing behavior set that will excel your performance beyond that of those around you and provide you with the tools necessary to take control of your life in the workplace and at home in order to create balance and fulfillment.

As mentioned before, behavior modification is not easy. For that matter, effective time management is not easy. However, if you are truly a high achiever and have faith in your ability to succeed, you will be able to permanently modify habits such that effective time management is a natural ability. Before long, effective time management habits will become a reflex, and then you will understand the true power of time management.

According to psychologists, it takes several weeks of continual corrected performance to permanently modify a behavior, and then continued practice to keep the behavior a habit. When trying to develop a new behavior, it can be difficult to stick with the effort, because old habits can be very hard to break. However, you are a high achiever, and as such you have what it takes to make a commitment and stick with the program until you succeed. To make the process easier, this guide presents a series of stages that will assist in the successful implementation of your behavior modification program.

If you choose to follow in detail the steps in this program, you will succeed in dramatically improving your time management.

"Should you find yourself in a chronically leaking boat, energy devoted to changing vessels is likely to be more productive than energy devoted to patching leaks."
Warren Buffett
CEO, Berkshire Hathaway

Chapter 1:

Action Plan

B efore going any further, you must make the commitment to improve your habits by precisely following each of the steps presented in this time management program. Without that commitment, I suggest you not waste your time reading the remainder of this guide, as it will do you no good. The choice is yours:

- I choose to diligently pursue this self-improvement effort to effectively manage my time.
  (Read on and begin the improvement process)

- I presently do not have the commitment necessary to complete this program.
  (Close this guide now, and come back when the commitment is there)

Congratulations on choosing to embark on this effective time management self-improvement process: you will not be disappointed with your decision as long as you remain committed.

The first step in the process is to take the commitment and enthusiasm you have right now and transform it into a tool that will hold you accountable for your performance. This step is called the action planning process. We will use the action planning process several times throughout the behavior modification program. Please use the blank action plan form to record your personalized entries.

Effective Time Management Action Plan

This action plan is a necessary tool used in my self-improvement effort to manage my time effectively. I am committed to this effort and this action plan will assist in holding me responsible for my performance.

My supporters are a critical part of this action plan. I require them to be very honest with me and to hold me accountable for my actions. In doing so, they will be helping me to achieve success in this effort to improve my life.

"The critical ingredient is getting off your butt and doing something. It's as simple as that. A lot of people have ideas, but there are few who decide to do something about them now. Not tomorrow. Not next week. But today. The true entrepreneur is a doer, not a dreamer."

Nolan Bushnell
Founder, Atari, Inc.

Objective What do you want to achieve?	
Goal What specific behavior do you want to address, and how do you want to address it?	
Action What specific action will be taken to modify your behavior to achieve the goal listed above?	
Target Date What date will performance be measured?	
Measures How will performance be measured to reflect specific performance results?	
Support Who will help me in this effort? What resources will I need for this effort?	
Status What is my performance?	

Objective

The action plan begins with recording what it is you wish to achieve.

Objective What do you want to achieve?	Example: *Effective Time Management*

Goal

The second step in designing the action plan is to record the specific behavior you want to address along with how you want to address it. It is important to be very specific so that there is no confusion about the intention of the action plan. If you feel it is necessary to complete numerous action plan forms to address the specific goals you have, please complete several action plan forms. The more specific you are, the better your performance will be.

Goal What specific behavior do you want to address, and how do you want to address it?	Example: *Successfully implement and complete each process step in Effective Time Management for High Achievers.*

Action

The third step in designing the action plan is to record the specific action that will be taken to modify your behavior to achieve the goal. Again, the more specific you are the better your success will be. It may be necessary to list numerous actions to achieve a single goal. It is perfectly acceptable to have several actions for a single goal as long as there are measurements *(recorded in step five)* for each of the actions.

Action	Example:
What specific action will be taken to modify your behavior to achieve the goal listed above?	*1) Read, understand and absorb all the Chapter 1 information.* *2) Complete the action plan for the time management self-improvement process.*

Target Date

The fourth step in designing the action plan is to record the date(s) that your performance will be measured. It is crucial to the process that this date be realistic. High achievers are notorious for selecting deadlines that can be overzealous: this is not a good tactic when dealing with self-improvement efforts. Choose deadlines that take into account potential delays and the involvement of others. Try to make your deadlines as realistic as possible while still holding yourself accountable for immediate and continual action.

Target Date	Example:
What date will performance be measured?	*1) One week after opening the guide = Time, Month, Day, Year.* *2) One day after successfully completing action #1 = Time, Month, Day, Year.*

Measures

The fifth step in designing the action plan is to record how your performance will be measured. The measurements must be quantitative and objective in order to retain validity throughout the behavior modification program. The measurements must also be specific and detailed. Please take the necessary time to develop a strong measurement system as your performance with the behavior modification program relies on it.

Measures	Example:
How will performance be measured to reflect specific performance results?	*Example:* *1) I am quizzed on Chapter 1 content and understand all key concepts.* *2) My action plan is complete and my supporters understand the plan and have agreed to participate.*

Support

The sixth step in designing the action plan is to determine who will help you in your self-improvement effort. Try to involve people that will hold you accountable for your performance and provide you with guidance when needed. The people in your support system do not necessarily have to be good time managers themselves; they simply need to be able to observe your performance on the goals set forth in your action plan.

It is also necessary in this step to determine what resources you will need in order to achieve the action plan goal. Resources such as finances, equipment, software, cooperation, etc. should be listed in detail.

Support	Example:
Who will help me in this effort? What resources will I need for this effort?	*Example:* *People to hold me accountable: my supervisor Chris, my family, Charlie, and Pat.* *Resources needed: new files, scheduling software, personal data assistant, desktop in-box.*

Status

The last step in designing the action plan is to record your performance. Using the measurements listed in the action plan, assess your performance on the target dates listed. The results, whether positive or negative, are recorded on the action plan and shared with your supporters.

Status What is my performance?	*Example:* *1) Chapter 1 quiz resulted in complete understanding of the chapter.* *2) Action plan is written however supporters have not given commitment to help.*

If you have not already done so, please complete an action plan for your overall commitment to being an effective time manager. Do not continue until your action plan is complete.

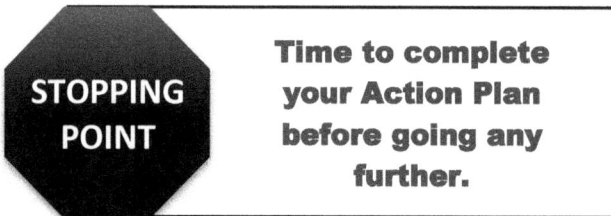

STOPPING POINT

Time to complete your Action Plan before going any further.

Chapter 2:

Habits

N̶ow that you have committed yourself to improving your time management skills, you are ready to participate in the next tool in the process to developing an effective time management system. This tool is split into two parts:

1) Report your current time management performance.
2) Assess your time management habits.

You may wish to use an action plan, similar to the one generated in Chapter 1, for one or both of these functions.

Report your current time management performance

Everyone has developed a set of time management habits that influence their daily activities to a level beyond that which they would like to admit. By reporting your own habits, you will be able to use them to your best advantage without needing to entirely rework your current time management approach. It is beneficial to make smaller changes to your schedule since it will be easier for you to comply with the necessary changes.

Reporting your current time management performance is simple if you are committed to the effort. It is crucial that this process is not shortcut in any way. The entire reporting process will take five days to complete, and must be completed as a series of five consecutive days. If there is a break in the reporting process, please start over again until five consecutive days are recorded.

Remember your commitment to creating a personalized time management system that will improve the quality of your life? This chapter will be testing that commitment. I know you want to move on and create the changes necessary to manage your time better, but my experience has demonstrated that this step is crucial to the success of the overall time management system. Stick with the process as described and you will experience the benefit of the time and effort invested.

The process is as follows:

"Our character is basically a composite of our habits. Because they are consistent, often unconscious patterns, they constantly, daily, express our character."

Stephen Covey
Author

Supplies Needed
- 1ea, letter size pad of lined paper with a left-hand margin
- 1ea, permanent ink pen

Process
1) Label the top page of your paper pad as "Day 1".

2) Near the top of the page in the left-hand margin, insert the label "Start of Day".

3) Starting with the top line of the page, record what it is that you are doing at the moment. Do not write down what you will be doing, or what you have just completed. Only record the task that you are performing at the moment. The task description should be very brief, try to keep it to only two or three words if possible.

4) Every time your task changes, record the new task on the next available blank line. Continue this process throughout the day, being careful to record all task changes. If you run out of room on the first page, please continue with a new page after putting an appropriate label and page number on it. Do not write on the backside of any page.

5) At mid-day, insert another label in the left-hand margin entitled "Middle of Day" adjacent to the task change occurring at the time.

6) Continue to record all task changes.

7) At the end of the day, insert the label "End of Day" in the left-hand margin adjacent to the last entry made that day.

8) Repeat the entire process with a new sheet of paper for Day 2, Day 3, Day 4, and Day 5…

Example: **DAY 1**	
Start of Day	Check voice mail and email
	Review customer letters
	Take phone calls
	Check in with project group
	Skim through trade journal
	Delegate project management
Middle of Day	Lunch with management team
	Follow up on special project X
	Design plan to improve processing system
	Teleconference with customer
	Meet with accounting
	Sort through mail
	Meet with vendor
End of Day	Meet for dinner

Do not continue with this guide until you have completed the five-day time management performance report.

STOPPING POINT

Time to complete your Action Plan before going any further.

Assess Your Time Management Habits

For this step you must have completed the five-day time management performance report. If you do not have five consecutive days of reporting, please start over again with the time management performance report before proceeding further.

With the data gathered in your report, you will be able to work with an objective party to determine your natural time management habits. Ideally, you will be able to use some of these habits to your advantage. It is important to be very honest with the analysis portion of this exercise. The objective party will help tremendously in holding you accountable for the assessment findings. Please try not to dispute your objective party: if they say it is so, it is probably true. You will need to accept the complete analysis findings as the truth before moving forward within the time management program. The analysis process is as follows:

Process

1) Set up an uninterrupted 20 minute meeting with your primary supporter. Let them know that their participation will be needed in helping you determine your natural time management habits, and that you will need them to be completely honest with their assessment.

2) At the meeting, lay out the five days of the time management performance report from left to right in consecutive order. If there are multiple pages for any of the days, tape the pages together making them one long page for each day. All of the pages should begin with "Start of Day" and should end with "End of Day" just like in the previous example.

3) Put together a brief list of five or six categories that you both agree upon that will describe the majority of the tasks you have listed in your report.

Example:

Special Project	*Financial*
Administrative work	*Organize*
Family	*Personal*

Most of the tasks listed in your report should fit one of the categories you agree to.

4) Design a matrix on the new paper that lists "Start of Day" "Middle of Day" and "End of Day" in the left-hand margin. The three titles should be evenly distributed down the left side page margin. On the right, make five columns beginning with Day 1 and ending with Day 5. The page should look something like this:

	Day 1	Day 2	Day 3	Day 4	Day 5
Start of Day					
Middle of Day					
End of Day					

<table>
<tr><td></td><td></td><td></td><td></td><td></td><td></td></tr>
</table>

5) Ask your participant to quickly review each day and make notes on the new page that describes your natural tendency to handle specific tasks at particular times of the day. For example, if there were several administrative tasks in the early-morning of Day 1, your participant would write in "administrative" at the Start of Day section of Day 1. Ask your participant to fill in the entire matrix with what they feel the general trend is for your task handling. Include things such as lunch breaks and rest breaks. Remember, do not dispute or correct your participant's assessment.

Example:

	Day 1	Day 2	Day 3	Day 4	Day 5
Start of Day	*Exercise* *Admin work* *File review* *Meetings*	*Breakfast meeting* *Organize* *File review* *Telephone*	*Exercise* *Admin work* *Telephone*	*Admin work* *Meetings*	*Filing* *Organize* *Delegate* *Telephone* *Meetings*
Middle of Day	*Lunch* *Telephone* *Special project*	*Lunch* *Telephone* *Meetings*	*Lunch* *File review* *Strategy*	*Lunch meeting* *Telephone* *Special project*	*Special project* *Telephone* *Golf meeting*
End of Day	*Park with kids*	*Movie*	*Organize* *Date Night*	*Dinner with family*	*Work on car*

6) Now ask your participant to use a new sheet of paper and assess the overall task management trends for the week based on the daily trend analysis.

Example:

	Overall Daily Trend
Start of Day	*Personal time*
	Administrative work
	File review
	Telephone
	Meetings
Middle of Day	*Lunch*
	Telephone
	Special project
End of Day	*Meetings*
	Family time

7) Your participant's input is now complete for this stage in the action plan. Thank your participant for their valuable input and let them know you may be asking them for additional assistance in the future.

At this point you have completed the assessment of your time management habits. The final summary assessment will be a valuable tool in helping to generate an optimal day plan as discussed in the next two sections.

Do not proceed to the next section until the assessment of your time management habits is complete.

STOPPING POINT

Complete the assessment of your time management habits before going any further.

Chapter 3:

_____

Energy

For this step you must have completed the assessment of your time management habits and have the summary assessment page in front of you. If you do not have the time management habit assessment, please complete it before proceeding.

With the data reported in your summary assessment page, you will be able to develop an optimized day plan that will assist in guiding your activities in the most efficient manner on a daily basis. Before the day plan is designed in detail, an energy curve assessment must be conducted and plotted out on a piece of paper.

Energy Curve

The energy curve is a scientific assessment of your individual level of energy on the average day. Every individual will feel more invigorated during certain times of the day than others. This is linked with human physiology and is completely natural. Once your energy curve is plotted, you will be able to make the appropriate adjustments to you day plan in order to take full advantage of the times that your energy is high and the times that your energy is low. The analysis process is as follows:

Supplies Needed
- Paper
- Pen or pencil
- Graphical spreadsheet or graphing software (optional)

23

Process

1) Set aside an uninterrupted 15-minute period for yourself to thoroughly assess your individual energy throughout the day.

2) Make a chart of the day that you can use to graph your energy level at each hour of the day. The left-hand vertical axis of the chart should be labeled energy level with a scale beginning with 0 at the bottom and increasing to 5 at the top of the scale. The bottom horizontal axis should begin with the 'Start of Day' time and end with the 'End of Day' time. For example, if you work from 8:00AM to 5:00PM, start the horizontal scale with 8:00AM, and then make a measurement point at 9:00AM, 10:00AM, 11:00AM, etc... through to 5:00PM.

3) Be very honest with yourself: make marks at the level of energy you have for each of the time measurement points throughout the day. A score of 0 would be no energy at all, and a score of 5 would be the most energy you have at any time of the day. After the points have been plotted on the chart, create a graph by connecting the points together with a line. You may wish to develop the graph using a spreadsheet or graph design program on your computer.

Example:

Your energy curve is now complete. The curve will help you to develop an organized day plan in the next section.

Do not continue to the next section without the completed energy curve.

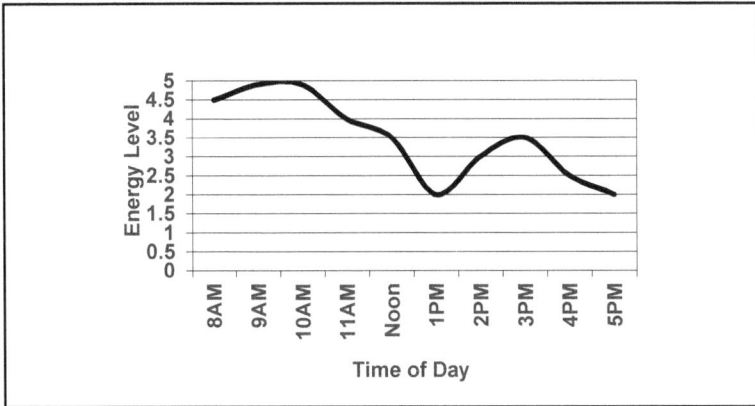

Energy Level vs. Time of Day

STOPPING POINT

Complete the energy curve assignment before going any further.

"Most people spend more time and energy going around problems that in trying to solve them."

Henry Ford
Founder, Ford Motor Company

Chapter 4:

Day Plan

For this step you must have completed the energy curve. If you do not have the energy curve, please complete it before proceeding.

With the data reported in your energy curve, you will be able to develop an optimized day plan that will assist in guiding your activities in the most efficient manner on a daily basis.

Because some tasks require a great deal of energy to complete efficiently and with quality, those tasks should only be performed during the time of day that your energy is high. Trying to complete an energy intensive task when your energy level is low will only create frustration, repeated review of your work, and procrastination. Conversely, many of the tasks that we perform are routine or procedural, and do not require a great deal of energy to complete with the expected performance or quality. These tasks can be completed during low energy periods because they do not demand intensified thought and may provide a much needed rest period in brain activity.

It is now possible to look at your energy curve and assign certain times of the day to generalized task categories. By assigning certain times of the day to specific task categories, you will expend your energy in a far more efficient fashion. You will also be able to group certain tasks together which will create further time efficiency. In addition, you can use your earlier determined time management habits to your advantage if they correspond with your energy curve. Once you have your day scheduled in a generalized format in accordance with your energy curve, you will have your day plan. The planning process is as follows:

Supplies Needed
- Paper
- Pen or pencil
- Spreadsheet or scheduling software (optional) (Examples: Microsoft® Excel®)
- Summary assessment of time management habits
- Energy curve

Process

1) Set aside an uninterrupted 30-minute period for yourself to diligently design your day plan.

2) Label each task of your summary assessment of time management habits with one of the following labels; high-energy, mid-energy, or low-energy. Make the determination based on how difficult the tasks are, how much attention you must give to each task, and the expected quality performance for each task.

3) Place your energy curve next to your summary time management habits assessment. Judge if there are any tasks that you have a natural tendency to complete at a specific time that may correspond with the energy curve. Make notes as you progress.

4) Begin to label each hour of the day with the most appropriate tasks to handle based on your energy curve and your time management habits. Don't be afraid to juggle various tasks around in order to find the best combination for the average day.

5) After the best combination has been achieved, generate an official day plan that you will be proud to display on your bulletin board or on your desktop.

"One of the greatest ironies of this age is that while various gadgets like smartphones and netbooks allow you to multitask, it seems that you never manage to get things done. You are caught in the busyness trap. There's just too much work to do in one day that sometimes you end up exhausted with half-finished tasks.

The problem lies in how to keep our energy level high to ensure that you finish at least one of your most important tasks for the day. There's just not enough hours in a day and it's not possible to be productive the whole time."

Prime Sarmiento
Life Coach

Example:

Day Plan

Special Project	Telep hone	Meetings	Lunch		Telep hone	Admin	Filing

Energy Level: 5, 4.5, 4, 3.5, 3, 2.5, 2, 1.5, 1, 0.5, 0

8AM 9AM 10AM 11AM Noon 1PM 2PM 3PM 4PM 5PM

Time of Day

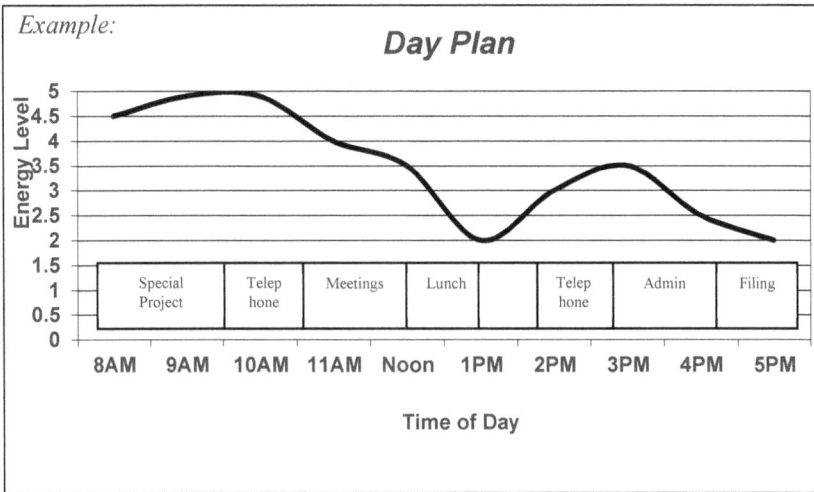

1) Post the day plan in a place that you will see every minute of every day. It is vital that this day plan be in plain view to remind you of the necessity of proper time management scheduling while your new habits are being built and reinforced.

2) Begin using your day plan to organize general tasks within the structure of the day plan for a minimum of five days. This will be difficult at first, but it will become easier with practice. This step is an excellent step to use the action plan format with!

Do not continue to the next section without first successfully scheduling general tasks in accordance with your day plan for a minimum of five days.

STOPPING POINT

Complete five days of scheduling in accordance with your day plan before going any further.

Chapter 5:

Scheduling

For this step you must have successfully scheduled general tasks in accordance with your day plan for a minimum of five days.

With the implementation of the day plan most individuals will begin to realize the amount of time that can be saved by effectively managing tasks by grouping them into categories and carrying out the tasks with the appropriate energy as dictated by the day plan. A typical participant in this process will already be realizing gains of two to five hours per week with very little effort. However, this is only the beginning!

The next stage in the self-improvement process will be to schedule all tasks no matter the difficulty or duration of the task. Sometimes this is confusing because most people are not accustomed to scheduling at a fine level of detail. In practical application, the finer the level of detail, the better scheduled you will be. Although this will most likely be very foreign at first, the benefits will quickly become apparent as you will find this method of scheduling will generate amazing levels of efficiency for you. The scheduling process is as follows:

Supplies Needed
- Scheduling software program (Examples: Microsoft® Outlook®, iCloud® Calendar, Google® Calendar Etc.)
- Smart Phone or Tablet computer that will download and upload to the software scheduling program above (not required but highly recommended)

- Day plan
- Brightly colored sticky notes
- Felt pen

Process

1) Set aside an uninterrupted four-hour to six-hour period for yourself to diligently schedule all of your tasks in accordance with your day plan. Close the door and let people know you are not to be interrupted. An off-hour time with nobody else around is an excellent approach to this exercise.

2) Accumulate all task folders, paperwork, notes, requests, reports, messages, and any other reminders that there is a task to be done. Put all of this information in a large pile in the middle of your desk. Make absolutely certain there is nothing left in an in-box, on the voice mail, or in a 'to do' file. All tasks must be in the pile of information before you can proceed. Resist the temptation to get discouraged. The pile may look ominous, however you are going to totally eliminate it in the next step. Furthermore, all of the tasks in the pile will be completely organized and scheduled so nothing will go unattended by accident and that should provide the confidence necessary to carry through with this process.

3) Using the brightly colored sticky notes and felt pen, make four category labels;

    a) urgent AND important
    b) urgent
    c) important
    d) neither urgent NOR important

Place the sticky notes on a desk or table with enough space between each to put a new stack of paperwork.

4) Take the top item in the pile of tasks and make a determination using the prioritization tool below. After a determination is made for the item, place it in the stack labeled with the appropriate sticky note. Continue in the same fashion for all the items in the pile of tasks. Resist the temptation to dig through the stack looking for other paperwork: take the top item and deal with it before you move to the next item. It is very important that you handle only one item at a time. Proceed steadily and methodically through the pile until there is nothing left in the pile and there are four stacks of information with each stack labeled with a sticky note.

> "The bottom line is, when people are crystal clear about the most important priorities of the organization and team they work with and prioritized their work around those top priorities, not only are they many times more productive, they discover they have the time they need to have a whole life."
>
> Steven Covey
> Author

HINT: To determine which pile to place the task into, use your vision and mission statement in conjunction with your core job duties to help make your decision easier. If it is a personal task, use your personal vision statement or visualize your preferred future to help make your decision easier.

| Urgent AND Important | Important | Urgent | NEITHER Urgent NOR Important |

5) Take all the information in the stack that is labeled neither urgent nor important and do one of two things with it: throw it away or delegate it away. You have no business handling anything that is neither urgent nor important. Get rid of it! If the tasks in this pile become urgent or important in the future they will come back to you, but for now, since they are neither urgent nor important, they do not deserve any more of your attention. Once you have thrown them away or have delegated them away, there are only three stacks of tasks left to schedule.

6) Because this time management process is new for you, you will not yet be scheduling routine meetings, updates, telephone calls, administrative work, or other repetitive tasks. First, you will be scheduling all of the items that need attention in order to clear up the time needed for the more repetitive tasks. Of course, you will still need to schedule time to handle your core job functions and personal responsibilities. If you must conduct a certain task at a certain time during a specific day of the week, put these tasks into your schedule at this time. Now use your scheduling software program to enter these tasks into your calendar and be sure to schedule enough time to complete the task so it will not have to be rescheduled later.

Example:
Payroll entry, every Thursday at 3:00PM to 4:30PM

---

7) Now that all the repetitive tasks that are required of your core job duties have been scheduled, you will begin to eliminate what remains in the three stacks of tasks. The first stack to eliminate will be the stack labeled 'urgent AND important' since these are most likely going to affect your performance, your organization's performance, or your personal relationships in a meaningful way. Take the first item off the top of the 'urgent AND important' stack, taking care to handle the item

only once. Make a determination as to how important the task is, and how long the task will take to complete. Using your day plan and your scheduling software program, find a time slot that is large enough to complete the task during the appropriate day plan category. If the task will take longer than the time allowed in your day plan, simply break the task up into multiple pieces and schedule more time on another day during the appropriate day plan category. After the task is scheduled, label a sticky note with the first date the task will be handled next (the date that you placed the task into your scheduling software program) and place it on the paperwork. Place the paperwork in a new stack labeled 'to be filed' that will be filed away in the next step. Remember to handle each item only once. Do not set it aside for later, or procrastinate about where to schedule the item. If necessary, there will be an opportunity to move the date and time of the scheduled task later in the process.

"Everything requires time. It is the only truly universal condition. All work takes place in time and uses up time. Yet most people take for granted this unique, irreplaceable, and necessary resource. Nothing else, perhaps, distinguishes effective executives as much as their tender loving care of time."

Peter F. Drucker
Author/Consultant

Example:

I have a financial statement that will be used in a comparative report I need to generate. It will take 20 minutes to complete the report and another 10 minutes to distribute it to the management team. This task must be done before the next management team meeting on the 10th, however it must include the financial information on the statement that I have as well as financial information through the 9th of the month.

I will schedule the task into my scheduling software program on the 9th between 3:00PM and 3:30PM because this is the time I have reserved for administrative tasks. However, I know that the more specific I am, the better my time management system will perform, so I will schedule two items into my scheduler. 3:00PM to 3:20PM will be used to generate the report, and 3:20PM to 3:30PM will be used to distribute the report to the management team.

I label a sticky note with "9th" and applied it to the paperwork I have, then I put the paperwork in the 'to be filed' stack.

To Be Filed

---

8) Move on to the next item in the 'urgent AND important' stack and schedule them similarly. Continue until all the items are scheduled in your calendar in accordance with your day plan. Resist the urge to overlap items into your scheduling software program. Initially, you may encounter too many things to do all at once, however this situation will quickly disappear as a result

of efficient time management. Remember that the tasks being scheduled are deliberately being scheduled with a specified time required for completion. Attempting to shorten the required time period or overlap tasks will do nothing but reduce the quality of your work. If there is not enough time to finish the tasks, do not blame the schedule as it is simply matter of having too many tasks to perform and something has to give.

9) After the 'urgent AND important' stack is eliminated, move on to the 'important' tasks since these are the next most likely to affect your performance, your organization's performance, or your personal relationships. As before, simply go through the stack one item at a time and schedule the tasks into your calendar using your day plan as a guide, taking care to handle each item only once. Remember to label each task with a sticky note with the first date the task will be handled next (the date that you placed the task into your scheduling software program) and place it on the paperwork before placing it in the 'to be filed' stack.

10) Next, schedule the 'urgent' stack. Chances are that your mindset will have changed a little by this time and many of the 'urgent' items may be declassified to 'neither urgent NOR important' status: if so, delegate the task or throw it out. In any case, handle the item only once just as you handled the previous stacks.

You should now have nothing left in the 'neither urgent NOR important,' 'urgent,' 'important,' and 'urgent AND important' stacks. All of the tasks should be labeled with the date of the next action to be taken, and all of the items should be in one big stack at labeled 'to be filed' this point. Do not continue to the next section without first successfully scheduling all of the tasks into your scheduling software program in accordance with your day plan guide.

STOPPING POINT

Complete scheduling all tasks before going any further.

"Your ability to select your most important task at each moment, and then to get started on that task and to get it done both quickly and well, will probably have more of an impact on your success than any other quality or skill you can develop."

Brian Tracy
Author

Chapter 6:

Organizing

For this step you must have successfully scheduled all tasks and labeled them with dated sticky notes.

You are probably feeling a bit overwhelmed and anxious at this point. It can be frightening to realize how much time is needed to complete all your scheduled tasks at a quality level and incorporate family time and personal time as well. Most people discover that there seems to be far too many tasks to complete, appointments to attend, and personal obligations to attend to; and much too little time to complete them. However, now that all your tasks are scheduled with appropriate time to complete them, and at the time of day that you will be more efficient, you can feel confident that they will be completed more quickly than they would have been without your time management effort. While your scheduled tasks may be completed late, they will eventually be finished and future tasks will not suffer the consequence of delays, inaction, and procrastination.

Because you are now scheduled, it is an excellent time to notify your coworkers, supervisors, friends, and family of the anticipated completion date of your tasks and promised appointments. A word of warning, not everyone will be happy to find out that his or her expectations will not be met. If this happens, kindly remind them that you are not inclined to sacrifice quality for timelines, and if they need the task completed earlier than scheduled you will need additional resources. This type of communication is foreign to the high achiever, as high achievers rarely ask for help or understanding when it comes to their own needs. Therefore you can rely on the comments being well received by others, and not interpreted as an excuse, because when the comments are coming from you they will be acknowledged as truth. If you tell your coworkers, family and friends that you are too busy to handle everything at once, they may not like hearing it, but they will believe you and respect you for being honest with them. Your coworkers, supervisors, friends, and family are just as aware of your high achiever attitude as you are; they will not think you are making excuses for poor performance or lack of interest.

Now that all the tasks are scheduled, it would be convenient to be able to locate those tasks easily and efficiently. This chapter will describe a tremendously effective method of organizing tasks, projects, documents, and correspondence.

Supplies Needed
- File cabinet within reach of your workspace (electronic or physical)
- Hanging files with label tabs (or electronic folders)
- File folders
- Felt pen

Process

Continue using the four to six-hour time period commitment made for scheduling. You will need about one hour in order to set up an organization system and file away the stack of tasks you have from the prior chapter.

1) A filing system must be set up to accommodate the new level of document organization. If you are primarily using electronic folders, it is still recommended that you use the guidelines communicated herein. Depending on how much paperwork you must process in an average day, you may wish to have an individual 'To Do' folder for each day of the calendar, or have

an individual "To Do' folder for each week of the month. This is a decision that you will need to make for yourself. For example, if you need to process 20 pages of new material each day, a separate 'To Do' hanging folder for each day would be appropriate. However, if you process 5 or 10 pages of new material each day, a 'To Do' hanging folder for each week would likely be appropriate. Make labeled 'To Do' hanging folders to identify the day, or the week, of the month. Also include a labeled 'To Do' file folder, which will slide into the identically labeled 'To Do' hanging folder, for each day, or week, of the month. This 'To Do' file folder can accommodate single pages or small documents that do not justify their own file folder. Install all of your empty 'To Do' hanging folders and file folders into a filing cabinet that is located within reach of your workspace.

To Do Files

Example 1:

    I have 10 new pages to process each day.
    I will make 4 hanging files labeled as follows:

To Do $1^{st} - 7^{th}$	To Do $8^{th} - 14^{th}$	To Do $15^{th} - 21^{st}$	To Do $22^{nd} - 31^{st}$

    each identifying a week of the month.

Example 2:

I have 20 new pages to process each day.
I will make 31 hanging files labeled as follows:

To Do 1st	To Do 2nd	To Do 3rd	... and so on...	To Do 31st

each identifying the day of the month.

Be creative with the filing system. Feel free to design a file system that suits your specific paperwork needs. The only criteria are that each file is labeled with the day or week of the month.

2) If you have many tasks that are bounded by some commonality, it may be helpful to split these tasks into their own subsection within the filing system. Using differently colored file folders can easily create specialized filing sections that can be used for routinely processed paperwork such as invoices, quotations, or requisitions, or keep track of personal training efforts, weight loss charts, or theatre and sporting tickets. If you use this method of sectioning tasks, be sure to keep the 'To Do' folders in addition to any new specialized folder generated. The new specialized folders should be labeled with the title of the common task, such as 'Quotes 1st - 7th' or something similar.

3) Once all the empty hanging files and file folders have been labeled and installed into the filing cabinet, take the top task from the filing stack and file it away in the appropriate file. You can tear off the sticky note at this time and throw it away. Continue with all of the tasks until there is nothing left outside of an organizational file.

4) Now close the drawer to your file cabinet and relax for a moment. Close your eyes and take a deep breath, then open your eyes and realize that there is nothing left for you to do, except for the things that you have already scheduled and

organized for your undivided attention at a later date. Isn't that a tremendous feeling of relief? Your workspace is clear of clutter, and all of your responsibilities are scheduled with a time of day that you will be able to accomplish the tasks most efficiently. Remember this feeling; for if you can stick with this time management program you will feel this way all the time. If you do not have the feeling of relief, and instead feel as if you cannot possibly get all the tasks done, please go back and start to schedule your tasks again, this time focusing on being specific and honest about your ability to complete the tasks at hand.

All of your tasks should now be scheduled and organized and there should be nothing remaining that needs to be attended to in any way until your first task that is scheduled in your calendar. This is critical to your success in this time management program. Do not proceed without first scheduling and organizing all tasks in your filing system.

STOPPING POINT

Complete organizing all tasks before going any further.

Chapter 7:

Staying Current

For this step you must have successfully scheduled and filed all tasks; there should be nothing remaining that needs to be attended in any way.

Staying current is the most difficult thing to do for the high achiever. The natural tendency is to attempt to please everyone all the time, which means taking care of a coworker or supervisor issue immediately regardless of the consequences, or committing to help out a friend when family time has already been promised. In reality, this type of behavior does nothing but reduce your overall performance by creating a haphazard schedule in which everything gets started and very little gets finished. This is tantamount to you being managed by your demands, rather that you managing your own demands. This fire-fighting behavior must stop now. Although there will undoubtedly be a period of adjustment for yourself and your peers, the net benefit will far outweigh the minor short-term inconveniences realized as a result of your behavior modification effort.

Supplies Needed
- Commitment
- In box
- Support by way of accountability

Process

1) Review your time management action plan to refresh your commitment to the behavior modification program. The change process will benefit you and those around you to an immense degree, but you must stick with the program. Because you are a high achiever, you <u>can</u> stick with this program; but only if you want to.

2) At work, put an in box on your desk. Make sure to label the in box so your coworkers know its purpose. Position the in box near the corner of the desk that is closest to the path that your coworkers travel to see you or drop things by. If your coworkers have to reach across your desk to put something in the in box, they will probably drop the item on your desk instead: that defeats the purpose of having an in box in the first place. Your in box will be the only route by which any task or paperwork will enter your schedule, it is important that it is used effectively.

3) At home, designate an area in the home as the place where all new plans, requests, tickets, and documents will be placed. Inform your family that anything that needs your attention must be placed there to insure it receives your consideration.

4) Schedule a fifteen-minute meeting with your action plan supporters. At the meeting let them know of your progress with the day plan, your scheduling and your organization. If you are enthusiastic about the progress, they will be too. Once they are in the encouraging and supportive mindset, let them know that you will need their help for the next several weeks in order to successfully accomplish the next step in your time management effort. Ask them to support you by delivering all tasks and paperwork to your in box. Let them know that you will be concentrating on effectively handling your scheduled tasks, and you will be working on avoiding distractions. Ask them to help you avoid distractions by letting you know if they see someone interrupting you with a non-critical item. Ask them to help you

by communicating with you through notes, voicemails, emails, and scheduling brief appointments rather than communicating when passing in the office hallways. Ask for their cooperation in understanding that you will be doing everything possible to avoid dealing with any item that is not written down or formally communicated. They will understand when you explain that the simple action of their taking a few seconds to write a simple note will ensure that you give their important issue your undivided attention rather than forgetting what it was they had asked. Most importantly, ask them to hold you accountable for your time management effort. Ask them to get involved and make sure you are scheduling your tasks according to your day plan. Ask them to check in with you every day to find out if you are following your time management program. More than anything else, this process makes your participants a part of the process and eases their concerns with your new behaviors. A similar meeting can be held with family and close friends.

5) Accept no tasks unless you receive it in writing, on a voicemail, or in an Email. If it is not an official form of communication or delegation, the task is not important. If someone insists on communicating only verbally, ask him or her if this is a formal request for you to take action, and then write down the request while you are standing there in front of him or her. In other words, take their time to write down the task, and then have them confirm that the task you wrote down is correct. Over time, this method will help them to change their behavior when dealing with you.

6) Use your in box for every item being brought to your attention. All the tasks, notes, mail, magazines, paperwork - everything! Picture the in box as a gateway to your world: all must pass through the gateway or it does not belong to you and does not deserve any of your attention.

7) Schedule ten minutes or so, two or three times a day, when you will go through the in box and schedule all of the tasks. Avoid

the temptation to schedule things as they arrive in your in box. Handle things only once, that means if you pull an item out of the in box, you will handle it, throw it away, delegate it, or schedule it. Depending on your job description, it may be necessary to glance at the new items in the in box to make sure there is nothing extremely urgent and important. However, if nothing fits that description, do not pull anything out until the prescribed scheduled time to go through the in box items.

8) Stick with the program. It will be extremely difficult at first, but it will become easier as time goes on and as you are able to handle your tasks with much greater efficiency and far less anxiety. Handle the tasks in your schedule at the prescribed times. Fight the urge to handle something else first: you will be happy once you have completed that difficult task that has been scheduled for a few days. Resist the urge to take on the easy tasks first and commit to strict compliance with your schedule.

9) Once your task is completed - delete it in your schedule! Close the book on the task. This feels wonderful! Get rid of the reminder that it needs **to be done**, because **it has been done!**

10) Fight the temptation to relax your time management efforts as things go smoothly. It is commonplace for high achievers to begin to relax their efforts as they find they have more free time each day. The time management system **is** the reason for the free time: to relax your efforts now would mean starting all over again, with the time management effort, once things fall apart. Do not relax your efforts. Stay committed and you will succeed in building new and improved time management habits.

At this point you should have an in box with all tasks, paperwork and inbound items being delivered through it. You should also be scheduling tasks according to your day plan two or three times per day. The support of your coworkers and family should also be holding you accountable for your time management efforts. If any of these things are not in place, go back and review the process until all factors are working for you.

STOPPING POINT

Review your performance and make corrective actions before going any further.

"The weird thing is that the more efficient, on task, on goal you are with your time, the more energy you have. Working with no traction, or for that matter simply wasting a day, does not relax you, it drains you.

Strange as it may seem, when you work a daily plan in pursuit of your written goals that flow from your mission statement born of your vision for living your dreams, you are energized after a tough long day."

Dave Ramsey
Author

Chapter 8:

Prioritize

Congratulations on successfully integrating basic time management for high achievers into your life. It is now time to learn advanced techniques and skills that will boost your time management efficiency even further.

This is the first stage of advanced time management. You should be a master of the previous steps before proceeding. If you are uncomfortable with any of the prior steps, please practice those steps first until proceeding with this chapter. It will not help your time management effort to proceed with this chapter if you are not a master of the basic time management steps. You are not expected to have developed any time management habits as yet; however if you are not practicing the processes as described in this time management program the remaining chapters of this guide will not benefit you.

Prioritization is a tool used to help manage tasks within your schedule. Correctly prioritizing work allows you to efficiently handle the most important tasks for your career and personal life. Effectively prioritizing tasks will also eliminate many tasks that you simply do not need to perform because they are not important to your goals. A high achiever with excellent prioritization skills will become a star performer for any organization because their time is spent on the important issues, not the routine busy work. Furthermore, those same prioritization skills will simultaneously allow the high achiever to create a fulfilling personal life.

Supplies Needed
- Organization's mission statement, vision statement, value statement, or other materials that clarify the important drivers for the high achiever's business affairs
- Job description
- Personal mission statement, vision statement, value statement, or other materials that clarify the important drivers for the high achiever's personal affairs

"If you don't prioritize your life, someone else will."

Greg McKeown
Author

Process for Business Affairs

1) Develop a reference tool for your organization's priorities. This list should be generated from the mission statement, vision statement, value statement, or any other materials used to clarify the important drivers for the organization. If your organization does not have these tools, set up a meeting with your organization's President/CEO to get the information directly from top management. Do not get the information from anyone other than the highest level of top management accessible.

2) Cross-reference the list of your organization's priorities with your job description. Develop a new list of primary job duties that are directly linked to your organization's priorities. The first item should be the most important factor. This new list is how you directly impact your organization's future and performance. If you excel at these items, you will be a star performer. Develop a list of primary job duties that you can refer to on a daily basis when making decisions on which tasks are most important to your performance and your organization's performance.

3) Cross-reference the list of primary job duties with your personal mission statement, vision statement, or value statement. These lists should match closely: if not, it may be time to consider another career path. High achievers can only truly excel if they believe in what they are working for.

4) After you have a comprehensive list of priorities, develop a refined list and publish it in a document that you can display at your desk, and take with you on business trips. Be creative and make something you are proud to display. Business card sized priority lists are terrific tools for the high achiever. Other ideas include mouse pads, screen savers, posters, desk pads, note pads, magnets, etc. The idea is to keep your personalized set of priorities in front of you at all times.

5) Use the list when you are scheduling tasks. Run through the list from top to bottom. Schedule those tasks that fit within priority

#1 first, and then continue through the list scheduling items appropriately with their priority. This process will ensure that the top priority items are never overlooked.

6) Tasks that do not correlate with any of the priority items are probably unimportant. Make a decision to delegate them or throw them away. It is not worth your time to invest in any task that is not related to your personalized priorities. If you feel you must address the task, although it is not related to your primary job duties, clarify with your supervisor that the task should be your responsibility and confirm the priority for the task to be completed. In this way, you are effectively amending the task into your priority list. Be sure to update your priority list as things change.

This prioritization tool will feel strange at first, but will quickly grow into a habit. Everyone around you will notice an improvement in efficiency and performance.

Process for Personal Affairs
1) Develop a reference tool for your personal priorities. This list should be generated from the mission statement, vision statement, value statement, or any other materials used to clarify the important drivers for your personal affairs. If you do not have these tools, set up a meeting with your family and talk about what factors are most important in family life. Clarify the expectations that each family member has of one another. Decide, as a family, how everyone will behave in order to achieve their desires within the family. If your family is willing, conduct a complete Life Planning Session that is discussed in detail in another of my publications.

2) Develop a list of primary personal duties that are directly linked to your family's priorities. The first item should be the most important factor. This list is how you directly impact your family's future and happiness. Develop a list of primary family

duties that you can refer to on a daily basis when making decisions on which tasks are most important to your family.

3) After you have a comprehensive list of priorities, develop a refined list and publish it in a document that you can display at your desk, at home, and take with you at all times. Be creative and make something you are proud to display. Business card sized priority lists are terrific tools for the high achiever. The idea is to keep your personalized set of priorities in front of you at all times.

4) Use the list when you are scheduling tasks. Run through the list from top to bottom. Schedule those tasks that fit within priority #1 first, and then continue through the list scheduling items appropriately with their priority. This process will ensure that the top priority items are never overlooked.

5) Tasks that do not correlate with any of the priority items are probably unimportant. Make a decision to delegate them or throw them away. It is not worth your time to invest in any task that is not related to your personalized priorities. If you feel you must address the task, although it is not related to your primary family duties, clarify with your family that the task should be your responsibility and confirm the priority for the task to be completed. In this way, you are effectively amending the task into your priority list. Be sure to update your priority list as things change.

This prioritization tool will feel strange at first, but will quickly grow into a habit. Your family will notice increased involvement from you and a more fulfilling family life.

At times the high achiever can feel overwhelmed with requests from business and/or personal obligations. It is during these times that time management efforts must be maintained at their most efficient. This can be extremely difficult because periods of overwhelm tend to create frantic thinking and difficulty in prioritizing. However, there is a brief tool that will help the high achiever prioritize tasks so they can be scheduled appropriately. The tool is called The Prioritization Tree.

The Prioritization Tree is designed to minimize uncertainty when multiple factors seemingly carry the same importance. Clarity is achieved by eliminating multiple factor decisions down to just one simple decision between any two items on the factor list, no matter how large the list.

"I learned that we can do anything, but we can't do everything... at least not at the same time. So think of your priorities not in terms of what activities you do, but when you do them. Timing is everything."

Dan Millman
Author

Chapter 8

Example:

Factors		Priority
A	*make deposit at the bank*	
B	*schedule the project*	
C	*read the mail*	
D	*pay the bills*	

What is more important: [Read factor **A**] or [Read factor **B**]? (circle the answer)
    What is more important: make a deposit at the bank or schedule the project?
    Factor A is more important than Factor B, so A is circled on the tree
What is more important: [Read factor **A**] or [Read factor **C**]? (circle the answer)
    What is more important: make a deposit at the bank or read the mail?
    Factor A is more important than Factor C, so A is circled on the tree
What is more important: [Read factor **B**] or [Read factor **C**]? (circle the answer)
    What is more important: schedule the project or pay the bills?
    Factor B is more important than Factor C, so B is circled on the tree
Continue for each decision point, and circle the answer. <u>Read the factors aloud each time.</u>

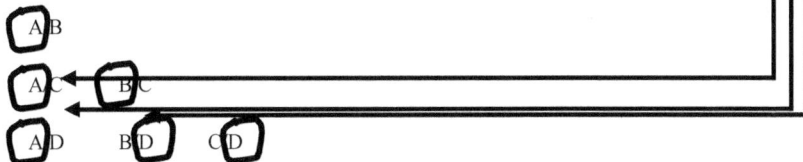

Once all the factors have been read aloud and a decision has been made between all, total up
the letters representing the factors.

A	B	C	D
3	*1*	*0*	*2*

Sort Factors from highest score to lowest score:

A	D	B	C

Insert priority into Factors table:

Factors		Priority
A	*make deposit at the bank*	*1st*
B	*schedule the project*	*3rd*
C	*read the mail*	*4th*
D	*pay the bills*	*2nd*

The next page contains a blank Prioritization Tree Worksheet

Prioritization Tree Worksheet

Factors		Priority
A		
B		
C		
D		
E		
F		
G		
H		
I		
J		
K		
L		
M		
N		

A/B

A/C B/C

A/D B/D C/D

A/E B/E C/E D/E

A/F B/F C/F D/F E/F

A/G B/G C/G D/G E/G F/G

A/H B/H C/H D/H E/H F/H G/H

A/I B/I C/I D/I E/I F/I G/I H/I

A/J B/J C/J D/J E/J F/J G/J H/J I/J

A/K B/K C/K D/K E/K F/K G/K H/K I/K J/K

A/L B/L C/L D/L E/L F/L G/L H/L I/L J/L K/L

A/M B/M C/M D/M E/M F/M G/M H/M I/M J/M K/M L/M

A/N B/N C/N D/N E/N F/N G/N H/N I/N J/N K/N L/N M/N

Totals:

A	B	C	D	E	F	G	H	I	J	K	L	M	N

Sort factors from highest to lowest score and insert factor priority here

Chapter 9:

Productivity Hour

Congratulations! If you have had the persistence to stay with this behavior modification program to this point, you are reaping many of the rewards of effective time management. High achievers following the program in detail are usually reporting an additional four to eight hours of productive time per week. While this is a tremendous benefit, there is still room for improvement.

As you are aware, high achievers seldom give themselves the chance to slow down and collect their thoughts. This trait can be hazardous to an effective time management program. It is well worth the effort to regularly stop and review performance and assess the results.

The productivity hour will provide a regularly scheduled time period for you to review your schedule, take care of your personal business, and to provide some 'think time' to catch up on all of those great ideas that have not been implemented yet. After all, now that you have discovered several hours of time per week, shouldn't you be using that time to your ultimate benefit?

Process
1) Schedule one hour per day that will be uninterrupted, call this time your 'productivity hour'. Try to schedule the time toward the middle of the day and when your coworkers, clients, and family are less likely to interrupt you. Schedule your productivity hour for at least one-month in advance so you will not be inclined to schedule anything else during this period.

2) Send a memo or email, or schedule a meeting to inform your coworkers that you will not be available for anything other than critical organizational issues during your productivity hour.

3) Do not accept any new tasks, meetings or unsolicited telephone calls during your productivity hour. Be firm about enforcing your productivity hour. You will find that using this time for your own review and 'think time' will generate creative ideas that will improve your performance beyond anything you have experienced before. The productivity hour is a key factor in truly using an effective time management program to benefit yourself and your organization.

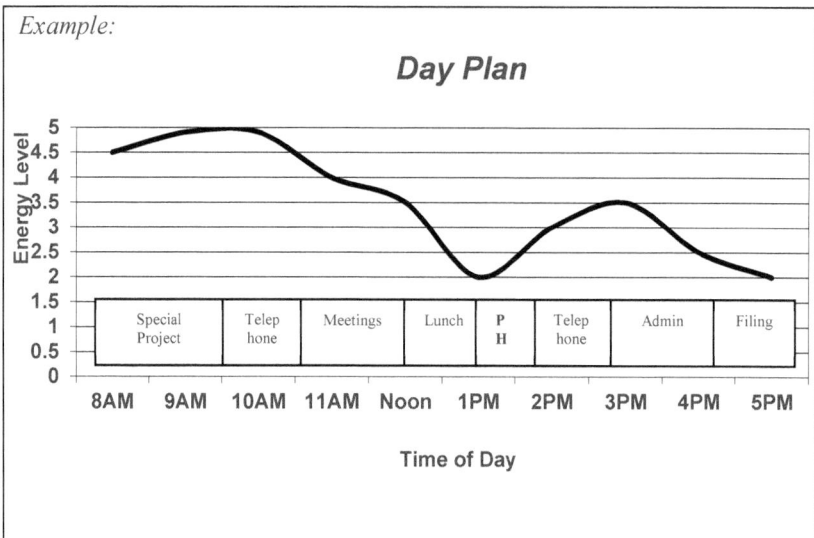

Example:

Day Plan

Time	8AM	9AM	10AM	11AM	Noon	1PM	2PM	3PM	4PM	5PM
Activity	Special Project	Telephone	Meetings	Lunch	P H	Telephone	Admin	Filing		

Energy Level (y-axis: 0, 0.5, 1, 1.5, 2, 2.5, 3, 3.5, 4, 4.5, 5)

Time of Day

"Reduce your plan to writing. The moment you complete this, you will have definitely given concrete form to the intangible desire."

Napoleon Hill
Author

Chapter 10:

Interruptions

Interruptions are often the effective time manager's most severe problem. Not only do interruptions distract attention from the task at hand, they also provide an excellent reason not to do what is scheduled when the high achiever would rather procrastinate than perform.

Your time is yours; it is nobody else's. You have the option to use your time to the fullest, or choose to waste your time. The point is, you control your own time, and because you are in control it means that you do not have to put up with somebody else wasting it for you. If you are truly performing the primary duties of your job function and family responsibilities, and are prioritizing your tasks appropriately, you should feel absolutely no guilt for disallowing unproductive distractions. Because your schedule is designed to accomplish all the tasks you need to do for your organization and family, it is a forgone conclusion that anybody interrupting you from achieving success is a detriment to your organization and family.

At this stage in your behavior modification program you have effectively taken control of your schedule and organization. You have also effectively developed a system for determining the importance of tasks and the order in which they will be completed. You have also invested the necessary time to be a contributing member of your organization and family through 'think time'. It is now the time to make the final commitment to take control of your entire schedule.

Process

1) If individuals interrupt you in the workplace try using the following tactic. Most interruptions can be avoided by simply asking the individual leading the interruption to come back in 10 minutes when you can give them your undivided attention. Amazingly, most of the time the individual will never return because they will answer their own question or seek assistance from someone else. If they do return, make sure to get the task in writing as discussed previously, then put the task in your in box and deal with it the next time you schedule the in box items.

2) Urgent interruptions can be very distracting. Often times, urgent interruptions are not important. Try using the tactic above, if that does not work, take the time to show the individual interrupting how to figure out the answer on their own. This tactic does initially take some time to do; however it will eliminate future interruptions. Additionally, you may be able to use this individual as a delegation resource in the future if someone else has the same question: you will be able to send him or her to the individual already trained rather than handling it yourself.

3) Client interruptions cannot be avoided in many cases. High achievers that need to deal with the client as a priority for their job description find it is necessary to schedule for the interruptions. That means schedule extra time into each task item with the assumption that you will be interrupted on a regular basis to handle client needs. However, do not use this extra time to handle any priority other than client needs.

4) Unavoidable interruptions are a reality of the world in which we live. When these interruptions happen, simply reschedule the tasks that were previously scheduled and handle the unexpected urgent and important priority. This is a wonderful tool because it allows the high achiever to always feel confident that all tasks will eventually be completed. Electronic scheduling software

makes it simple to juggle tasks around when unavoidable interruptions do occur and cause a ripple in the schedule.

5) Interruptions can pile up at times. In these situations your previously scheduled time management efforts for the day can be totally destroyed. Do not allow this to depress you. Simply take ten minutes and regroup. Go through the tasks and reschedule them according to priority. Remember that you are always in control of your time management efforts: even when situations seem out of control.

6) Stay focused regardless of an interruption. Several methods of dealing with interruptions have been outlined here. You probably have your own set of tactics as well. Above all, stay focused on the task at hand rather than trying to do a dozen things all at once. The only thing that happens when you diversify your attention is to delay the completion of all the tasks simultaneously. Take care of one thing at a time and focus on it until it is complete. If you cannot complete the task, then schedule another time to complete the task at a later date.

7) Allow only one project on your desk at a time. Distractions caused by paperwork stacks and project files can be worse than individuals interrupting you. Get all that paperwork off your desk so you can focus on the project at hand. The only items on your desk should include the task being worked on; everything else should be scheduled and filed away, or in your in box waiting for your next in box review.

Chapter 11:

Commitment

As mentioned in the beginning of this guide, many high achievers have tremendous success with this time management program. If you are not encountering similar results there are only two possibilities. First, you are already an excellent time manager. Second, the commitment to make this life-altering change is not there.

There is nothing to be ashamed of if you simply do not feel the need to improve your time management performance to the level of a star performer. For most people the pressure associated with being a high achieving star performer is overwhelming and is not beneficial to their mental health or personal lives. However, if you are serious about making the most of your time and abilities, this commitment must be given the utmost effort. It is not an exaggeration to state that effective time management will impact every part of your life - forever. Imagine making an extra four hours a week for your family: over the course of one year that will add up to 208 hours!

Keep your commitment strong. Revisit the action plans developed throughout this behavior modification program to remind yourself of the effort needed to succeed. Do not get lazy with time management efforts, even if things seem to be going extremely well. Time management is a continual effort - you will never be able to stop consciously prioritizing, scheduling and revising. This is a lifetime commitment.

If you stray from the program you can get back on the program within a couple of hours. Simply follow all the steps we have gone through from the beginning of this guide. Know that this time management effort will benefit your life to great levels. Know that you will be a better performer as a direct result of this time management program. You will be successful.

"Objectives are not fate; they are direction. They are not commands; they are commitments. They do not determine the future; they are means to mobilize the resources and energies of the business for the making of the future."

Peter F. Drucker
Author/Consultant

Chapter 12:

Rewards

As you know, this time management program is not easy. It is a serious behavior modification program for high achievers that are serious about their success. Not everyone can master this system. However, the high achievers that do master the program are star performers.

Performance deserves rewards. When you accomplish the behaviors of the effective time manager, you should be rewarded as well. Already you will be rewarded with more productive time and the feeling of being in control of your schedule. You will also be rewarded every time you have the opportunity to delete one of those tasks that was just completed. While these rewards are terrific and ongoing, perhaps it would be a prime opportunity to really give yourself a reward for making the commitment and sticking with this very difficult program until your behaviors are changed permanently. After all, this is a life-changing program!

Wouldn't it be a great idea to set a goal to affect permanent change in your time management behavior? An action plan with measurements to determine lasting results would be an excellent tool for proving success in this regard. Perhaps this is the perfect opportunity to reward you performance with a family vacation, a new car, or perhaps a fantastic new gizmo you have had your eye on for some time.

Reward your success: you deserve it. You have achieved a level of productivity that most people will only dream about their entire lives. Congratulations to you and may you have many more successes in your future. Of course, you are bound to have many more successes now that you are an effective time manager.

"Greater even than the pious man is he who eats that which is the fruit of his own toil; for scripture declares him twice-blessed."

The Talmud

www.ingramcontent.com/pod-product-compliance
Lightning Source LLC
LaVergne TN
LVHW021622080426
835510LV00019B/2709